Bug Out:

PREPPER PREPARATIONS FOR SURVIVAL, SHTF, NATURAL DISASTERS, OFF GRID LIVING, CIVIL UNREST, AND MARTIAL LAW TO HELP YOU SURVIVE THE END TIMES

By: Tom Eckerd

Special Request

Thank you for purchasing our book and supporting our Ministry. We have a Special Request for those that have purchased this book on the Kindle platform. We wanted to make you aware that Amazon's Kindle platform pays per pages "read". Our Special Request is that if you appreciate our Ministry's efforts to put out books such as this or if you would simply like to support our Ministry's work to please scroll to the back of the book, even if you don't "read" the book right away. This is how we will get paid through the paid per pages criteria.

We all lead such busy lives nowadays and can get side tracked so easily please take a moment to support us now by allowing us to be paid by scrolling to the end of the book – Then go back and read it at your leisure.

We deeply appreciate Your support and know that God will Bless You as You have Blessed this Ministry.

Dedication

This book is dedicated to the watchmen of God who faithfully watch and pray as Lord commanded all of us to do and to my Lord and Savior Jesus Christ who continues to lead, guide and protect us as we move forward in courage and faith to shine the light into the darkness.

Forward

This book is written to help the average person learn what is necessary to survive SHTF, Natural Disasters, Off Grid Living, Civil Unrest, and Martial Law to Help You Survive the End Times. This book gives solid advice and strategy to help keep you and your family safe in even the worst situation.

The title of this book is, "Bug Out". When I write, "Bug Out" it is a call to action to those that have eyes to see and ears to hear. What I mean is that is it time right now to Bug Out and to do so in a permanent way. I encourage everyone reading this book to get off the x as fast as possible for we are fast approaching the time in history that will never be forgotten.

Table of Contents

Chapter 1:
Financial Considerations

Here's the harsh reality - You won't be able to buy or sell anything without taking the Mark of the Beast when it comes out. For Christian Preppers we know what's coming, but how many of us have actually thought about what that really mean in practical terms? In practical terms you have to plan to be homeless before you are in fact homeless and without money. Accepting the Mark of the Beast is simply not an option for true Christians so you need to have a solid plan in place prior to it's implementation.

Until the Mark of the Beast is thrust upon us attempt to gain as much money and resources that you can and storing it in "Key Locations" - NOT in Banks. I strongly recommend working online and staying mobile as well.

Anthony Fleischmann put out a great book called, How To Finance Your Full-Time RV Dream. I strongly recommend everyone checking out this book as it gives great insight as to how to stay on the move and work remotely both online and off - a true must have book no doubt.

It is possible to spend thousands of dollars trying to get ready for a Bug Out. I have seen people spend thousands of dollars getting prepared and they're still working on more. Some families have moved their families to safer areas, bugging out and getting off the grid before anything can happen.

Clearly, you can spend a lot of money preparing to Bug Out. But that doesn't mean that you HAVE TO spend a lot of money. Actually, the more Survival Skill you know, the less you need to spend. People without those skills have to spend more money, because they can't survive without the necessary survival gear.

Learning survival skills is a good investment of your time. Not only will it save you money, but it will also increase your family's chances of making it through when you choose to Bug Out. Knowing what to do is at least 80 percent of the battle and having the stuff to do it with is the other 20 percent - Keep those numbers in mind.

For the Christian Prepper, there is one other factor, which is important to remember - The Lord. More than anything we need to count on The Lord to take care of us once we have done what we could do.

When the children of Israel were passing through the desert God took care of their needs. Yes, they had to gather the manna and the quail, and they still had to cook it; but God made sure it was there. If you do your part God is surely to do His.

Note how the Israelites dependence on God didn't preclude their leaving Egypt well prepared. Before they left, they were commanded to go to their neighbors, asking for gold and silver. They were told to take all their livestock with them (food). They went into the desert prepared to stay and never return. The largest bug out in history; and while they went prepared, they depended upon God for their true provision. That's a balance we need to emulate.

Our God is a God of provision. Most people are aware of the verse, *"But my God shall supply all your need according to his riches in glory by Christ Jesus."* (Ph 4:19). But knowing it and living it are two different things - this is where you need to have courage and faith. Don't allow fear to beat out your faith - if you can't trust the Word of God in this, how can you say you really trust it about Salvation? Trust in the Lord with all thine heart; and lean not unto thine own understanding (Proverbs 3:5)

The thing is, in this sort of situation, you're going to have to depend on God for most everything, or you aren't going to make it - this is especially true regarding your finances or provisions. That deer that wanders into camp so that you could kill it... God sent it. That rain that fell so that you could refill your water jugs... God sent that too. Yes, by all means, do your part; but in the larger part, depend on God and He will take care of you.

Our part is in the preparations, we need to build our bug out bag and be ready to go. That raises the question, how much will that cost? If you look at some commercially available bug out bags on the market, you can easily spend two or three thousand dollars on them. But that doesn't mean you have to. My bug out bag, with the equipment in it cost me less than $500, not counting weapons, a bow, my coat and fishing gear. I already had those things and the price on them can vary considerably.

I've seen bug out bags that people have made, which cost them less than $100, but I didn't choose to go that route. When you look over the list of equipment in my bag, you can see that it is heavy on survival gear. I could have gone cheaper, by not bringing as much. But I made the decision to go heavy on equipment, in order to increase my chances of survival.

The other expensive item to consider is your supply caches. Depending on how much you put in them and what you choose to put in them, those will probably cost you somewhere between $60 and $120 each. That price is for the ones in a 5-gallon bucket. Of course, a large cache will run more than that, perhaps several hundred dollars, once again, depending on what you put in them. Just take it step by step in an organized way so you have what you need when you need it.

Chapter 2:
Considerations for Families

Bugging out is difficult for anyone. The challenges of getting away from home, coupled with living in the wilderness off of what God provides in nature can challenge the best of us. But bugging out with a family takes what is typically a difficult situation and adds whole new dimensions of problems.

Even Jesus recognized this and made mention of it when he was talking about bugging out. I quoted His statement from Luke earlier, but he also talks about it in Matthew. There He says:

> *And woe unto them that are with child, and to them that give suck in those days! 20 But pray ye that your flight be not in the winter, neither on the sabbath day:*

> *Matthew 24:19-20*

Anyone who is a parent knows that raising children is a challenge. But could you imagine trying to raise children in conditions that require you to bug out? Not only would you have to do all the normal things you would do at home, but you'd have to provide for them in less than ideal circumstances, while protecting them from everything that nature can throw at them as well as the evil of man.

Yet you can't abandon your children. God has entrusted them to you for a purpose, so you have to plan for them and plan how you are going to take care of them in those circumstances. This is critical, because failure to plan is usually the best way to ensure failure.

To start with, you need to prepare your children for the eventuality of bugging out. That means a little bit of physical conditioning, so that they can walk a long distance, as well as preparing them mentally for the idea of leaving home and living out in the woods. You can make this much easier for them by simply taking the time to do just that; go spend time in the woods training them in various aspects of survival.

Camping is a great opportunity to teach the necessary skills for wilderness survival, without having the risks associated with having to survive. You can teach your children how to make a shelter, how to start a fire, how to purify water, how to fish, how to build a snare and a host of other skills, all under the guise of going out to the woods and going camping for the weekend. Actually, you'll need several weekends, but the more the better.

Make sure you include some good hikes as part of those camping weekends. Let them carry their own pack, all be it a small one. That way, they can get used to the physical strain of it, as well as the idea of walking for several hours. The more you do, the more they will be strengthened and prepared.

Don't forget to teach your children how to shoot, either. Children can actually start shooting rather young, if they are responsible enough to understand gun safety. Start them light, with a .22 caliber rifle and work up from there.

No matter what happens, they will undoubtedly need the ability to use a firearm, both for hunting and self-defense. Things will get that bad in the future no doubt.

Keep in mind that children will slow you down in your travels. How much they slow you down will depend a lot on their age and physical condition. Babies will slow you down because you have to carry them or take them along in a stroller. As your children grow, they will gradually become better conditioned and better prepared to hold up their own end of the work, becoming useful members of your survival team. As teens, you should be able to teach them to the point where they can survive on their own.

When planning your escape route, do so with the limitations of your children in mind. It is quite possible that you will only be able to travel three or four miles a day, not the 10 to 20 you could make alone.

You also need to plan on teaching and training your children, once you are out in the wild.

Their education is important, especially to their future survival. Even if the world as we know it comes to an end, they will need skills to live and make a living.

A strong family can survive together. There's a reason why God created the family unit, and that reason is for the children. As parents, we are charged with the responsibility of preparing the next generation, with the idea that they will go farther than we have and accomplish more than we do. Only you can do that; nobody else can do that for you - So prepare them well.

Chapter 3:
How To Start Preparations

Before you start doing anything, you need to make sure your head is in the right place. As believers in Jesus Christ, everything we do must come out of faith, not fear. Why is that? Because when we walk in fear, we allow the devil to have control of our lives, but when we walk in faith, we put God in control.

This idea of walking in faith is so important, that Paul told the Romans that anything they did, without faith, was actually sin:

> *And he that doubteth is damned if he eat, because he eateth not of faith: for whatsoever is not of faith is sin.*

> *Romans 14:23*

One could easily ignore that verse, because it is in the midst of a trestle about eating food offered to idols. The verse itself talks about that as well. Since that isn't part of our culture, we might think it doesn't apply. But the important part is the last seven words, "whatsoever is not of faith is sin." This can be seen as the opposite side of Hebrews 11:6:

> *But without faith it is impossible to please him: for he that cometh to God must believe that he is, and that he is a rewarder of them that diligently seek him.*

> *Hebrews 11:6*

So the first and most important part of our preparation has to be getting our thoughts in order. We must *"Cast down imaginations and every high thing that exalteth itself against the knowledge of God..."* (2 Cor 10:5). While there are many things which we could talk about which could fall into this category of "imaginations" or "high things," there is one which I am sure qualifies, that is fear.

Praise God that we don't have any reason why we need to operate in fear. While we have the capacity for fear, we are not committed to it in any way. Any fear that we have, did not come from God.

> *For God hath not given us the spirit of fear; but of power, and of love, and of a sound mind.*

2 Timothy 1:7

Okay, so it's clear that we should not be preparing for a crisis situation because of fear. Does that mean we should ignore those situations altogether? No; we should prepare out of love, specifically a love for our families and a desire to take care of them. God has entrusted them to us, and while we depend on Him for provision and all our needs, we are not called to just sit on the sofa and watch television. We are called to work and prepare.

One of the really great things about preparing out of love for our families, is that it helps to protect us from fear. Love and fear are incompatible. When one is in operation, it prevents the other from working:

> There is no fear in love; *but perfect love casteth out fear*: because fear hath torment. He that feareth is not made perfect in love.

1 John 4:18

So get your love going. Take action based on that. As long as you keep yourself operating in love, you won't be operating in fear. Your love and your focus will protect you from fear entering in and taking control of you.

That's all fine and dandy, but what's the first step?

As in many things, the first step is knowledge. You've got to have an idea of what it is that you need to do, before you can take action and do it; otherwise, all you're going to do is waste a lot of time and money. Fortunately for you, you've taken the first step. Buying this book is setting you on the road towards preparedness.

Of course, you need to take action on the things you learn from this book. Preparedness is not just a mindset (although that is an important part of it), but a whole series of actions. Your actions will determine how prepared you are and how well you are able to do, once a true disaster strikes.

Don't let your learning stop here either. This book will help you prepare to bug out, when that time comes, but it doesn't discuss how to survive in the wilderness. You need to learn a whole new set of skills, so that you are ready to survive and keep your family alive, when the time comes to bug out and go to the mountains.

Chapter 4: Caching

Caches? What in the World are Caches; is that like a peanut? No, No that a Cashew. If you are still reading at this point you may know what Caches are, but how much do you really know? One common mistake for Preppers to make is to keep their entire stockpile in their home, in one location or in one cache. On one hand, that makes sense, as most people plan on bugging in during a disaster, rather than bugging out.

But on the other hand, having everything in your home or one location means that in the case of a disaster that destroys your home, or in the case of a mob attacking your stockpiled location, you lose everything you have – And the wife is not going to like that one bit, especially when she most likely put up with your crazy prepping for so long. Now when it's needed the most it's not there – Yeah, definitely not going to go over well.

That's why supply caches are so important. They spread your supplies around, putting them in convenient places where you might need them. That's way, no matter what you end up having to do to survive, you have some supplies readily at hand. Now these supplies will not be very extensive most likely but will give you what you need to survive.

To accomplish this, you need caches in multiple locations. While that is more work, it will ultimately serve you better to have several different caches, which you can access, rather than just one – And the wife can be happy. Basically, you want to break your caches down into a few basic areas.

Near your home – If you are bugging in, you want extra supplies that you can access readily. These caches also serve if your home is broken into and your supplies are stolen or your home is destroyed and you need some ready supplies. Local storage units are great for this – But think Creatively

Your workplace – If you own your own business or you have some storage space available at your work, you could create a small cache there. That would provide you with supplies for yourself and your co-workers, if a disaster leaves you trapped at work for a few days.

Your bug-out location – This is probably the most important place to have caches prepared. You probably won't be able to take everything you need with you, so by having caches at or near your bug out location, you ensure that you will have supplies available. If you own that location, you can stock it well, but if not, you'll need to find someplace to hide your caches.

Along your bug out route – The average bug out bag only has three to five days worth of food in it. But if you have to go on foot, you may need many more days to get to your survival retreat than the food you are carrying. Putting a couple of caches along the way allows you to re-supply. You should do this every 3-5 Miles, especially if you're traveling with children.

Combat Caches – This is something you should consider wisely and as I must mention in accordance with all local, state, and federal laws. Combat Caches are designed to give you a tactical advantage and could be stocked with a multitude of items that include things like sealed ammo, parts to firearms, knives, etc. – Just use your imagination but stay within the law. Combat Caches should be placed in a tactically advantageous location such as high ground, rocky terrain, vantage points, etc.

As you can see, properly placing a cache requires considerable forethought. You need to pick locations that are going to work out well as part of your overall survival plan. Not just anyplace will do. But where do you actually make the cache?

One of the best locations I've run across for a survival cache is a rented storage locker; the kind that has sprung up all across the country as people's possessions outgrew their storage space. You can rent small spaces the size of a closet, for a minimal monthly fee, which is enough space to set up a pretty good cache.

Another option is to establish one at the home of a like-minded friend or family member, if they have space. Of course, they'll have to be someone you can trust.

The other possibility is to bury your caches.
This is best for the ones along your bug out
route and may also be best at your bug out
location. Plastic five-gallon buckets work
well for this, as they are water-tight, can
hold a fair amount and are readily available
at all home improvement centers. You can
also use PVC pipe, but that won't hold as
much.

If you bury caches, make sure that you have
multiple landmarks to locate them by. Don't
use trees for landmarks, as they can burn
down or be cut down. Instead, use features
of the landscape, such as rock outcroppings.
Those are permanent, short of removing
them with heavy equipment or dynamite. If
that becomes the case, you'll probably lose
your cache anyway.

You can put literally anything in a cache, but the basic idea is to use them for food, ammunition and basic survival equipment.

You should already have your survival equipment with you, so the only reason I'm mentioning survival equipment is in case you lose yours or can't get to your bug out bag. Other than that, the biggest item is food, as that's what you'll be consuming the most of.

Creating Supply Caches

There's no way that anyone can carry all the supplies they'll need for a prolonged stay in the wilderness. A typical bug out bag only has three days of rations in it. If you do it like I do, then you'll have five days worth. But even that's not enough, and you really can't carry more. Weight limitations are going to control how much you can fit in your pack.

Now, if you're Grizzly Adams, that won't be a problem, because you'll just be able to live off the land. But then, Adams lived a few hundred years ago, when there were fewer people in this country and much more wild game. The prairies are no longer covered with buffalo as far as the eye can see and even deer, which are by no means nearing extinction but are not as plentiful as they once were.

So, you're going to have to have supplies to live off of, especially food. While you will probably be able to augment your food supplies somewhat from nature, you can't really count on that too much, especially at the beginning. There's no way you can count on it for the majority of your needs. Since you can't carry it and you can't hunt for it, you're going to have to get food from other people. That means, buying it ahead of time and creating caches of food that you can access when the time comes.

Notice that I say "caches" and not "cache." You really don't just want one cache. There are several problems with having only one cache, top amongst them being that others could find it and you could lose everything.

Any cache needs to contain an assortment of your most critical supplies. That mostly means food, but should also include:

- Toilet paper
- Personal hygiene supplies
- Medical supplies
- Fishing supplies
- Ammunition
- Matches
- Vegetable seeds

The food in your caches should be lightweight, high energy, with about a 20 percent protein content. If you are bugging out into an area where game and fish will be plentiful, you can lower the protein content a bit; but make sure you have some. For high energy, concentrate on carbohydrates, which your body can break down into simple sugars to provide energy.

You may also want to consider adding clothing to your caches, especially if you have growing children. You'll need clothes for them, when they outgrow the ones they'll be wearing when you bug out.

A five gallon plastic bucket makes a great cache, as it can be filled, sealed and buried, without any risk of the contents being destroyed by moisture, animals or insects. The bucket itself will be useful as well for a variety of tasks around your survival retreat. If you need more space, you can use multiple buckets or you can use 55 gallon drums. The only problem with the drums is finding ones with removable lids.

Your best bet is to bury your caches in the wilderness. Make a ring of them a few hours walk around your expected bug out location, so that you can reach them fairly easily. Place some along the route as well, so that you have some source of resupply while you are traveling. If you have to travel on foot to reach your bug out location, you'll need resupply before you can get there.

The hardest part of this is remembering where you left your cache. If you are burying them, they will be extremely hard to find. Make sure you pick good landmarks, which won't change.

Many people pick trees, but those are some of the worst landmarks you can pick. Trees can be destroyed by forest fire, killed by disease or cut down by other people. Better to pick things like rock outcroppings, which won't change with time.

Another option is to rent a storage space in a rural town that is nearby your bug out location. This could be a larger cache, but by no means should be your only one. The advantage here is that it doesn't have to be buried. But depending on the reason for your bug out, you may not be able to access it.

Keep in mind that you will never be able to retrieve everything that you have in your caches. Things will happen. Some sites will be destroyed by construction or nature herself. You'll lose your ability to find others. Events may keep you from going to even others. So, you ultimately want to have more caches than you'll need. That way, you can be sure of having enough.

Chapter 5: Bug Out Bag

When the time comes to bug out, you're going to need equipment and supplies to survive; that's where the bug out bag comes in. You're not going to be able to go to someplace where you can pick up a loaf of bread and a gallon of milk at the corner store. Nor are you likely to find an abandoned cabin in the woods, with a welcome sign hanging on the door. You're going to have to live off of what you take with you, the knowledge you have and what nature provides - if that scares you, you need more training.

So, it's best to take as much with you as possible, specifically the things that will help you survive out in the wild. Of course, that means knowing how to use those things to survive with as well. Ultimately, the most important thing you can take with you is the knowledge of how to survive.

The bug out bag must provide for all of your basic needs, so it would be a good idea to review what those are. In order of priority, your needs are:

- Maintaining your body heat (this includes clothing, shelter, and fire)
- Purified / Drinkable Water
- Food
- Self-Defense
- First-Aid (including personal hygiene)

Carrying all of that is going to be a bit difficult. You have to assume that you're going to have to go on foot at some point.

Even if you leave home in your car or truck, chances are that you'll have to abandon it along the way. With that in mind, you need to make your bug out bag something that you can realistically carry, such as a backpack.

When selecting a backpack, try to avoid something that is obviously military in appearance. That's too easy to identify as what it is. You don't want people to realize that you're bugging out or recognize that you're prepared. So, you're better off with a backpacker's backpack, rather than a military one.

You want to make sure that whatever backpack you pick has a weight-bearing belt. Your legs are much stronger than your back, and can support the weight of the backpack and its contents easier than your back can. But if the pack doesn't have a belt, your back will have to carry the weight.

Most people have to limit their pack to about one-fourth their body weight. But that's assuming that you're in shape. If not, you'll have to make it even less. One way to compensate for this is to have every member of the family carry their own pack.

While women and children can't carry as heavy of a pack as a man can, they should be able to carry their own clothes, personal toiletries and sleeping bag, as well as some food.

Bug out bags are very personal, simply because each person's situation is unique. You need to match the pack you carry to your needs, the terrain you are going to travel through, the area you are going to set up camp and your own survival skills. There's absolutely no sense in carrying equipment you can't use, no matter how useful it might seem.

With that in mind, here's what you should include:

- Backpacking Tent
- Tarp
- Cordage (paracord is best)
- Duct tape
- Wire ties (useful for tying branches together)
- Backpacking sleeping bag

- One set of rugged, warm clothing
- Extra socks
- Coat (seasonally appropriate)
- Hat (also seasonally appropriate)
- Work gloves
- Rain poncho

Fire

- Fire starters (at least two primary - waterproof matches and a disposable lighter; and one secondary - BlastMatch, Metal Match or Ferro Rod)
- Fire accelerant (WetFire cubes are excellent, or you can make your own by working petroleum jelly into cotton balls)

Purified water

- Canteen or water bottle (minimum 1 liter, two are better than one) (each person)
- Water purifying straw (Lifestraw is best) (each person)
- Bag-type water filter (one for the family)
- WAPI - water pasteurization indicator (one for the family)

Food

- Enough food to last for five days (dried foods are best, lightest weight)
- Survival fishing kit
- Wire for snares
- Backpacking cookware set (each person)
- Backpacking cups and plates (each person)
- Backpacking utensils (each person)
- Camp stove (not essential, but can be useful)

Self-defense

- Firearms (each person who can shoot should have a pistol and a long gun)
- Extra ammo (caution, ammo is heavy)
- Bow (also good for hunting)
- Additional weapons (if you have family members skilled in their use)

First-aid

- Trauma first-aid kit (this is bigger than your typical family first-aid kit and designed for dealing with larger injuries
- Personal hygiene needs
- Anti-bacterial hand cleaner (great when you don't have water available)

Tools

- Camp hatchet (preferably with a built-in hammer)
- Folding pruning saw (for cutting wood)
- Folding saw
- Sheath knife (each person)
- Multi-tool (useful for multiple things)
- Tactical flashlight (each person, with extra batteries)

As you can see, this list is rather lengthy; but unless you are going to make everything yourself once you get there, you really need it all. Keep weight in mind on all your purchases.

When looking at things like backpacking tents and cookware, you're really paying for weight savings. The lighter it is, the more expensive it is. Don't skimp on quality, as your life and that of your family is riding on that equipment performing, as it should - This is not a game and you should remember that!

Try to buy items, which are multi-purpose whenever you can. That's a good way to save weight. There's an axiom in the prepping community, which has been taken from the military. It goes, "Two is one and one is none." That speaks of the need for redundancy. If something breaks or becomes lost, you'll need something you can fall back on. I cannot stress this philosophy enough. This is where "Proper Planning Prevents Problems" So Keep it Simple and Remember Murphy's Law(s).

Chapter 6: INCH Bag

An INCH Bag – That Sounds Tiny . . . . What is an INCH Bag?

A lot of bug out bags are based on FEMA's recommended list, from their emergency preparedness website. But that list assumes that anyone bugging out is going to head for their nearest FEMA "shelter" to ride out the disaster. Well, I don't know about you, but turning myself over to the government is not something that I'm willing to do.

That's why my Bug Out Bag is really an INCH bag. That means "I'm Not Coming Home" bag. Does that mean that if I Bug Out, I'm never coming back? To be honest, I don't know. But I pack that bag as if that's the case, because there's no way for me to know.

You've probably seen some of those movies about the End Times, where a small group of believers is hiding out from the government. Well, what would you need, if you were in that situation? A regular bug out bag wouldn't be enough, because you would be leaving home, with the idea of never coming back.

An INCH bag has to be heavy on survival gear, as it may very well contain all your worldly possessions, once you leave your home. If your home is destroyed and you are forced to abandon it, you could literally end up with that being everything you own. In that case, it needs to have everything you'll need while on the move.

What does that mean? It means that your INCH bag will contain enough tools and equipment that you can build a long-term shelter, start innumerable fires and filter your own water, as well as hunt and scavenge for your own food. At the same time, you're going to have to be your own doctor, provide yourself with clothing, make shoes and make anything else you're going to need. That's going to be one packed bag.

In reality, you can't fit all that in one backpack; at least, not and still be able to carry it. What you really need is more than one bag. The first one is your bug out bag, and it contains all your survival equipment. The second (and possibly third) bags will contain:

- Extra clothing
- Sleeping bags
- Ammo
- Hunting bow (with arrows)
- Seeds

Those contents are going to have to be able to help you start your homestead off in the wild. Seeds and a hunting bow are very important parts of this list, as they will give you the ability to feed yourself, without attracting attention. While a nice hunting rifle is easier to hunt with, it's also noisy. Bows may not have as long a range, but at least they're quiet.

You can build a long-term shelter with the tools you can carry in a Bug Out Bag, but it's gonna be hard. That's why I mention tools in the second bag. Those tools will be the tools you'll use to build a shelter. If you have the skills to use them consider the following tools list for specifically building a long-term shelter

Tools you may need to build a long-term shelter:

- Shovel
- Full-sized axe
- Bow saw or bucksaw
- Froe (for making shingles and splitting boards)
- Adze (for squaring tops and bottoms of logs for a cabin, as well as making furniture)
- Framing chisel
- Carpenter's crosscut saw
- Pick (for breaking up ground)
- Brace & bits (for drilling holes)

I realize that sounds like a rather extensive tool list and it represents a lot of weight. But if you're going to build a log cabin out in the woods somewhere, that's the minimum you're going to need unless your just that skilled with an axe and buck saw. As it is, you're going to do a lot of backbreaking work with those tools, in order to get your cabin built. If you leave anything out, you're going to have a much harder time of it. A great idea is to stash these items in a cache.

Chapter 7: Bug Out Vehicle

The Bug Out Vehicle – What's that All about? For many preppers, Bug Out vehicles are one of the "fun" parts of prepping. I mean, c'mon, who doesn't want a nice big four-wheel-drive pickup, all decked out for fun in the rocks and the mud? There's just something manly about that image, like an untamed stallion running across the prairie. We all want to be that one who catches and tames that stallion... or truck... or whatever.

But before you run out and sign a huge loan for that big truck you're wanting, let's stop and think about it for a moment. You want to be sure to get the right thing, especially on such a big purchase. New trucks are expensive, especially new four-wheel-drive trucks. Before you can even start picking out a bug out vehicle, you need to develop your bug out plan.

That means knowing where you're going to go, the triggers that will tell you it's time to go and how you're going to get there. Once you have that, you're ready to start thinking about your bug out vehicle.

Some people get real elaborate with their bug out vehicles, buying or building something that's more suited for the military, than for a family. While I like those vehicles as much as the next guy, I'm not sure that they're a practical selection for a bug out vehicle. Oh, they'll get you there... at least, if the crowd of people on the freeway don't stop you and kill you for your vehicle.

You see, stealth is an important part of Bugging Out, as important as mobility. You have to assume that other people are going to be Bugging Out at the same time and that traffic will get backed up.

When that happens, there's a good chance that some vehicles will run out of gas and others will overheat. Their owners will become desperate and start looking for anything they can find to help them out of the situation. In such a moment, your fancy 4×4 truck, could look like salvation to them.

The last thing you want to do is put yourself or your family in the position where you either have to kill someone or allow them to kill you. While that may end up happening anyway, you should try and avoid it at all cost. Again this is where proper planning will prevent problems from arising - Think it through.

Of course, a lot depends on where you live. In Texas, just about everyone drives a truck or SUV. So yours won't stand out.

But if you're driving that in New York, it probably will. So, pick a vehicle that will blend in and make sure it's in a color that won't attract attention.

The flip side of that coin is being able to go off-road, if you need to. There's a good chance that all those out of gas and overheated vehicles will end up blocking the highways. When that happens, it might be necessary to cut across some empty field or even some farmer's field, in order to get away. You're not going to do that successfully in your average family sedan.

Only you can analyze your escape route and determine if four-wheel-drive will really help you. If it won't then there's no real reason to buy it. You've got to balance that against your need for stealth, as well as thinking about how much space you need for your family and what you're going to take with you.

In all actuality, you probably already have a vehicle that you can use as a Bug Out vehicle. Maybe it won't be as good and maybe it won't be as sexy; but taking out a loan to buy a Bug Out vehicle, will prevent you from doing the other prepping you need, and that's a wise use of your money. Take the time to think it through and make sure that your plan ends up fitting your budget - Be Strategic!.

Chapter 8: Where To Go

Any bug out requires a destination. If you don't have any idea of where you are going, then all you are doing is running away. While there are times when that may be necessary, that isn't the way to ensure your survival. You need an integrated plan, which includes where you are going, how you're going to get there and what you'll do to survive at your bug out retreat.

Fortunately, the Bible gives us some guidance on this. It says,

> Then let them which are in Judea _flee to the mountains_; and let them which are in the midst of it depart out; and let not them that are in the countries enter thereinto.
>
> _Luke 21:21_

Of course, the problem with that is that we are not likely to recognize when we need to roll out. So, do we ignore that advice, assuming that whatever disaster is happening isn't the our line in the sand or bugging out isn't justifiable. You have to have your "Bug Out Triggers" predetermined and established for your entire family. This is where your courage and faith comes in, you either believe what you have been planning for and bug out or you don't. Your actions will clearly reveal the truth of the matter and if in fact you are a hypocrite.

But the real point I want to bring out here is the one about where we are to flee to. Jesus Himself gave some very specific instructions on that; He said to *"flee to the mountains."* Now, I don't really know why Jesus said that or why He chose the mountains.

But as an expert on survival, I can say that He made the best possible choice. But then, He knows everything, so that's not a surprise.

The thing is, there really is no better place to try and survive than in the mountains. Survival requires that you have the necessary resources. While you will be bringing some of those with you, you will have to rely on your caches to see you through. There's just no way that you can take enough supplies to last you the rest of your life. You're going to need to learn to live off the land if you don't already.

Living off the land is challenging. But living off the land in the mountains, where you are surrounded by forests, game and fish is much easier than trying to survive in the middle of a Kansas cornfield or in Urban death traps.

Everything you need is there, more so than anywhere else. Specifically, the mountains provide:

- Forests to hide in
- Wood for fire
- Building materials (trees and rocks)
- Animals to eat
- Fish to eat
- Edible plants
- Sources of water

Not only that, but the mountains will do a better job of hiding you from prying eyes than anywhere else. Sounds are deceptive in the mountains, with echoes and sounds bouncing down canyons. Even if you use a firearm to shoot game, someone looking for you would have a hard time to pinpoint exactly where you were. The short line-of-sight helps too, as it's difficult to look over broad areas, searching for a particular person or target.

Now, the Lord doesn't give us guidance as to which mountains we should bug out to; that's up to you and me. But don't wait until it's time to bug out, in order to select the mountains. You want to have a specific destination in mind; someplace you can get to in a reasonable amount of time, where you will have everything you need.

Ideally, you would be best off if you owned a cabin in the mountains and could stockpile supplies there. That away, when you bug out, you have some place to go, that's ready and prepared for you. But few of us can afford that at this point. You'll probably have to find a spot to go to and plan on building a shelter when you get there.

Joel Skousen has a wonderful book that can help you find someplace that would work as a bug out location. It's his book, "Strategic Relocation" the third edition. This new edition adds a whole lot of new material and new areas to what he had before. If you don't know where to go, I'd highly recommend it.

Chapter 9: How Do I Get There?

Most people think of driving when they think of bugging out. Some even go so far as to invest in massive four-wheel-drive vehicles, just for that purpose. That's not surprising though, considering that we are highly mobile society, which is used to taking a car wherever we go.

There's just one problem with that idea. If you're bugging out, there's a good chance that a whole lot of other people are going to be bugging out at the same time. That means that the roads will be crowded with people who are unprepared. They'll run out of gas and their cars will overheat, turning the highways into parking lots -then what?

If you have a 4x4 truck or SUV, you might be able to go around the traffic, heading out across country.

A lot will depend on where you live and what sorts of fields you will have to pass through. If you live in the middle of Texas ranchlands, there will probably be dirt trails you can take across country.

But if you live in the middle of New Jersey, you're not going to find that. So, before spending money on that vehicle, take a look at your route and determine whether it will help you or not but understand things can change rapidly.

You need to plan your route in detail, looking at road conditions, probable traffic problems and alternate routes you can take. As much as possible, find the back way to get there, preferably a back way that few others will know about. Avoid major highways, roads, intersections and bridges as much as possible.

If your route involves a highway, then know where you can get off that highway and take an alternate route. I'm not just talking about places where there are side roads either. Can you cut across some farmer's pasture? How about some power lines right-of-way? Don't limit your thinking to roads; think in terms of places you can get through with a vehicle, a horse or on foot.

Chances are, you're not going to be able to get where you're going in a car; maybe not even in a 4x4 truck. However, that's not to say that you shouldn't have plans to bug out in your vehicle; just that you consider other options as well. Go as far as you can in the vehicle, but be ready to abandon it at any time and continue on foot, man's oldest means of transportation.

Traveling on foot is difficult and slow. If your family is in good shape and your children are somewhat grown up, you might be able to make ten miles per day, walking. But if you're traveling with small children, don't expect to make more than three or four miles per day. A push cart can help with this, as you can put the children in it and push them along, saving time.

For that matter, a push cart can also be a way of increasing how much you can carry. You're limited with your bug out bag or INCH bag to how much you can carry.

But if you can use a cart, you can add another 100 pounds of food and supplies. That's well worth considering. Just make sure it has large enough wheels for the terrain you'll have to cross.

As you travel, you'll need to stay alert about everything that is going on around you. As some people say it, "Keep your head on a swivel." That a way, you can see behind you, as well as in front. There will be others traveling too, and the most dangerous predator on the face of the Earth is the two-legged one. You have to assume that anyone else you see is going to be a hostile and want to take what you have - including your life.

There are a lot of people who think that the law will be thrown out the window in a bug out situation. That's a dangerous way to think. Basically, it's the way the bad guys think.

But even if there is a breakdown of society with a breakdown of law and order, the rule of law will eventually be reestablished. When that happens, they may start to investigate various situations depending on just how crazy it gets. Avoid all drama as best as possible and you'll be good to go.

As I just mentioned, you want to avoid confrontations if possible. But if you have one, keep in mind that the law will still apply, even if there is nobody there to arrest you. The technical terminology is that it's legal to use deadly force for self-defense or the defense of others, as long you are in imminent danger of life or limb. Your defense of your actions has to be able to pass the test of reasonableness. That means a reasonable person taking reasonable action in the circumstances. If you can't demonstrate that, you could be charged with murder but each State's standard is different.

Chapter 10: Bug Out Retreat

A Bug Out Retreat – That doesn't sound like it makes sense. Preppers regularly debate the wisdom of bugging out versus bugging in, with the majority of experts coming down on the side of bugging in. But that's based on some very clear assumptions, especially the assumption that anyone bugging out is going to go live in the wild, trying to live off the land with nothing but what they're carrying in their bug out bag.

Based on that assumption, I'd have to say that bugging in is preferable. Living off the land is much harder than most of us realize. But that doesn't make bugging in an excellent idea, especially if you live in a big city. Even disasters such as a small hurricane can cause a breakdown in society, at least to some extent - just look at Katrina. If that's the case, then what's going to happen with a major disaster? Say, something nationwide?

The lawless element of society will grow and they'll be attacking anyone they can, in order to find the things that they need to survive. Being a Prepper around such people will become very dangerous.

That's why a bug out retreat is a superior option to bugging in. A bug out retreat gives you the option of leaving town and getting away from the two-legged predators, without having to put your family at risk. By pre-planning and preparing someplace to go, you can best protect your family. But there's another reason for us to bug out, rather than bug in. That is, Jesus gave us that commanded it. In fact, He tells us that in three of the gospels (Mt 24:16; Mar 13:14; Luke 21:21), which means it must be important. Specifically, He tells us to go to the mountains when we see the abomination of desolation. So, where are there mountains nearby you? This is the place to put your Bug Out Retreat.

Hold on, I can already hear you. There are some of you out there saying that you can't afford a bug out retreat. Maybe that's true or maybe you're just thinking of it the wrong way. Buying the land is usually the most expensive part. If you can get away from that part, you can take out a lot of the cost of building your bug out retreat. In fact, that opens a number of possibilities to you.

The first of these is to create it on property owned by a friend or family member who lives out of town. Perhaps their reason for living outside of town is that they want to survive. If that's the case, you can form a survival team together. Then, you can build a shelter on their property out of scavenged materials. Another option is to use a travel trailer. You can buy older used travel trailers for a couple thousand dollars. If you're the do-it-yourselfer type, you can fix that trailer up, making a nice shelter out of it.

Then you either keep it at home or find a good place to store it that would be conveniently close to where you plan on placing your bug out shelter.

Don't forget small towns either. Most of them will be much safer during a crisis than the big cities. But people who live in small towns will probably be suspicious of strangers. So, you will need to integrate yourself with that town beforehand, so that they accept you when you arrive. Regardless of the type of bug out retreat you create, the mountains are the best place to do it. Not only will you be well hidden from those two-legged predators, but the mountains provide an abundance of resources which you will need to have access to, in order to survive as we previously mentioned in this book.

Chapter 11:
I'm Here, Now What

Living in the wild is a complicated and difficult task; you've got to get pretty much everything you need directly from nature itself. In this, you need to understand your priorities and make sure that you work in alignment with those priorities. Failure to take care of everything in a meaningful, logical way could prove to be fatal, especially when you find that you don't have something critical that you need.

But before you start with any of your normal survival priorities, you've got to keep yourself alive. That means keeping yourself alive from the two-legged predators and anyone else who might be looking for you. If things are dangerous enough that you've decided you have to bug out, then I think it's safe to say that they are dangerous everywhere.

You'll want to do everything you can to stay out of people's sight as you are approaching your bug out retreat. The last thing you will want to do is lead them right to where you're planning on hiding out. So take the time to check your back trail carefully, looking for others who may be on it. Watch for the smoke from their campfires, look for colors that don't belong, listen for noise that doesn't come from nature and look for the flash of light from anything, as that's probably them.

High points are an excellent place for doing this surveillance along your back trail. When you stop at night and again before you leave in the morning, take a look from a high point. If you cross a ridge, stop there and do it as well.

When you are getting close to your destination, take a deceptive path, as if you are going around it or you are going to pass it. If you can, walk in the water for a ways, so that you don't leave a path. When you come out of the water, do so on a rock, so that there are no tracks for anyone to follow. Walk on rocks whenever you can; If necessary use deadfalls, but rocks are better.

Upon arrival at your bug out retreat, your first action must be to establish your perimeter security. Use the people you have at your disposal, your family or survival team, and keep some on guard at all times. Patrol the area, looking for bad guys or any sign of them passing near. Do everything you can to avoid leaving sign of your own. That means to walk without leaving tracks, breaking sticks or leaving threads from your clothes hanging from a bush.

Of course, you're going to have to integrate your self-defense tasks with your other survival tasks. It won't do you the least bit of good to protect yourself from dying in one way, only to succumb to it in some other. While those two-legged predators are dangerous, the biggest killer in the wild is hypothermia.

There are certain priorities, which are essential to survival. You've got to make sure you meet those needs, or you're just not going to make it. The top priorities are normally referred to as the rule of 3s:

- You can die of loss of body heat in 3 hrs
- You can die of lack of water in 3 days
- You can die of lack of food in 30 days

So, start by keeping yourself warm. That means setting up a shelter and starting a fire. You want to be careful with your fire, because a visible fire can be seen for miles at night. Likewise, smoke can be seen for miles in the daytime. So, you need to make sure that your fire is hidden by a stone fire pit and located under a tree, allowing the tree's branches to help dissipate the smoke. Use only dry wood, as it will smoke much less than damp wood will.

Your shelter must be hidden as well, regardless of what kind it is. Before building it, look around the area and pick somewhere that it will be hidden.

A building in the middle of a mountain valley makes it rather obvious that someone is living there. Better to hide it in the middle of the forest and plant brush and saplings all around it to hide it.

Use camouflage as much as possible for your shelter and for everything you do.

The idea is to blend into your surroundings and become invisible. The better you can do that, the less likely you are to be found. At the same time, you'll need to be active, hauling water, hunting for food, gathering plants and firewood, maybe even tending a vegetable garden. All that activity makes you vulnerable to being seen and attacked.

You can do a lot to hide yourself and your activities. Lean to move through the underbrush without leaving a trail or making noise. Moccasins are much better for this than boots, as they don't have a distinct edge like a shoe or boot sole does. But in order to have moccasins, you'll need to kill an animal and tan the hide.

Avoid using the same path over and over or you'll leave a visible trail to follow. When you get water, approach the water from a different direction every time. That way, you can't be ambushed as easily. Vary your routine and you'll make it more difficult for the bad guys.

Of course, you've got to stay armed at all times. Make your guns part of you. Your handgun should be on your person from the time you wake up till the time you go to bed. Whenever you leave your shelter, you should take your rifle or bow with you. That includes going 50 feet to get some water.

Your days living in the wild will be busy ones. There will be plenty for you to do, in order to keep yourself and your family alive. Be sure to use your time wisely, so as to get everything done. At the same time, stay alert.

As you learn the sounds and habits of the animals in the forest, they will warn you of anyone coming. That will become the best alarm system you could have, even better than what you can do yourself.

Chapter 12:
Alternative Housing

Now there are two options – Stay put and dig in or Bug Out. As we already clarified in a previous chapter God's plan is for us to Bug Out so we can avoid being a victim of circumstances. Have you ever realized that God always provides a way of escape for His people, whether it's an Ark, Rapture, or Mighty Man of God to lead His people – He always provides a way of escape.

Tiny Houses may seem to be the next Big Thing but are they right for you? Tiny Houses offer a lot of options but they are still stationary. I don't consider the Tiny Houses on Trailers actually Tiny Houses.

When I talk about Tiny Houses I'm talking about a small shed like building that is on the ground – just so we are on the same page here. It makes sense why so many people considering them.

Many are sick of the rat race and are actively taking steps to ensure their future survival both economically and beyond. It is absolutely possible to have a Tiny House built for 10-20k that has enough room for you and your family's needs.

If you put it on some land . . . . you're good to go. For some that might make a good Bug Out Retreat. Others might consider this option if they have special needs or situations such as an ill family member. However, if at all possible actively consider a mobile lifestyle – This is the Biblical example.

RVing Full-Time may be the way to go. I gotta say hitting the open road and not looking back does sound very appealing right now with the way our country is. I actually believe that the person who can do RVing full-time should do so. Author, Anthony J. Fleischmann Jr. has written an excellent book, "How To Finance Your Full-Time RV Dream". This book will teach you how to live a Bug Out lifestyle if you would. RVing full-time is Bugging Out permanently, and this is the best option until roads get locked down and travel restricted - at that point head to your bug out retreat.

I believe God calls us to use "Escape & Evasion" tactics in these last days when we will be hunted and killed in the 5th Seal. Start the process today by learning how to finance your full-time RV dream.

Chapter 13: Get Off The Grid

There are some people who are considering off-grid living and moving out into the country; either to live in a cabin in the woods or to establish a true homestead.

But what if we took that concept a step further? What if we could create an off-grid lifestyle for yourselves, in a home that's truly designed to be self-contained and for true off grid living?

What I'm talking about here is the ultimate bug out. But I'm not just talking about it as something to do when things go to crap and you've got to abandon your home; I'm talking about doing it now; making it your new lifestyle. I'm talking about buying a RV, and living in that before things get even more ridiculous in this country.

If you were living in a RV, you could spend most of your time in places where you would want to bugged out, away from the hustle and bustle of city life, as well as the dangers associated with being amongst a large number of people in the midst of social chaos, civil unrest or martial law. If a disaster happened, you wouldn't have to bug out, you'd already be bugged out - Now that's proper planning.

Believe it or not, there are already a fair number of people who live like this; people you may not normally see. Most experience a freedom that seldom is even comprehended by the majority of people out there.

Some are entertainers, working with circuses, carnivals and fairs. Others travel from trade-show to trade-show, selling their wares. Then there's probably the biggest group of all, retired people, who live in RVs so that they can travel and enjoy what's left of their lives.

They go north in the summer, when it's nice up there and south in the winter to avoid the snow. They visit family and friends, taking their home with them. In between time, they may stay at a campground, enjoying nature or the company of others who live the same lifestyle.

But you don't have to be retired in order to enjoy this sort of lifestyle. You can still work and be on the road at the same time, all you need is an Internet connection that is reliable wherever you go.

More and more companies are hiring freelancers to take care of everything from engineering tasks to writing, accounting to graphic arts.

If you have a skill that people need, you can find work through online agencies, connecting you with companies that will pay you as a freelancer, to do their work for them. With that, you can take your family on the road, working wherever you go and traveling between time.

There are a couple of factors which work in your favor, if you choose this sort of a lifestyle. First of all, your cost of living will be much lower than it is today. Assuming that you can sell your home with enough profit to allow you to buy a RV, your main expense is going to be gasoline. Many of your monthly expenses will disappear, allowing you to work less hours and still make enough money for your needs.

Another great advantage of this lifestyle is that it provides you with an excellent opportunity to teach your children real world survival skills.

There are countless campgrounds across the nation which are located in the woods. State and federal park campgrounds are the best for this. Pick a skill to work on in each campground and hone your family's survival skills as you go.

Then there's what I've already mentioned; the fact that most of the time you'll already be bugged out. As long as you keep track of the news, you'll know what's going on and what to avoid. So you should be able to avoid most problems. If it looks like a hurricane is coming into the Gulf Cost, and you happen to be in that area, all you have to do is move inland, before everyone else does. Pick a campground and settle in to wait out the storm.

The one drawback to this system is a lack of storage space in the RV. If you try and downsize from a home to an RV, you'll have to get rid of a lot of what you're used to using. That means that you won't have a lot of room for a stockpile of emergency supplies. However, if you plan properly, you can still bring several months along with you.

They can be in the under-coach storage, in roof pods or under beds. Or, you could bring along a cargo trailer to carry your stockpile.

Another option is to set up caches of supplies in various storage areas, in areas that you frequent. That a way, if things get bad, you'll always have supplies that you can access, as long as you can get to them. With several such locations, you should be in good shape, no matter what comes your way.

Chapter 14: What To Buy

A Basic Shopping List for Your BOB or INCH Bag

Basic Tools for your Bug out Bag or INCH Bag: Concept: Never rely completely on one particular item to get a job done!

- Back Pack
- Your Weapons & Ammo (a Ruger 10/22 or Shotgun is a Great Choice for general survival but will only help a little when dealing with the two legged bad guys – for that consider the AR15, AK, or SKS.
- Good Knife (The Best You Can Afford)
- Multi-Function Tool (Gerber or Leatherman)
- Folding Saw (Bahco Laplander)
- Bob's Quick Buck Saw (with extra blades)
- One Gransfors Bruks Axe
- Cold Steel Special Forces Shovel
- 550 Cord 300 feet and number 12 Bank Line (1lb spoil)

Shelter:

- Small 2 person Tent. This is actually a one-person tent with your gear. If you have a family plan accordingly. However, just remember to stay out of sight. Reusable Space Emergency Blanket / Tarp
- SOL Emergency Bivy – Green
- United States Military Bivy is another option. This is more durable but add a little more weight.
- One 100% Wool Blanket. Make sure it's actually 100% wool.

Fire Starting Equipment:

- Faro Rod
- Magnifying Glass
- Flint & Steel
- Metal Container holding Card Cloth
- Magnesium Block
- Matches in water proof container of some kind
- Lighters
- Cotton Balls covered in petroleum jelly
- Knowledge and Ability to start fire using primitive techniques.

Food:

- Cliff Bars (20 grams of Protein each)
- Organic Trail Mix
- 1 Mainstay Food Ration Bar (3600 cal.)
- 3-5 MREs (because you don't need water to cook them)
- Snares, Fishing Yo Yos, and two 220 Conibear Traps
- The Ability to catch, trap, or hunt game to secure a renewable food source as well as process it in the field. Don't forget to bring some zip lock bags. Learn how to smoke you meats to help preserve it.

Water:

- Purification Tablets
- Water Filter (Katadyn Pocket Micro filter)
- 1 Plastic fold-down 5 gallon water container
- 1 Steel cup/bowl for boiling water (Stanley put out a really good little kit)
- Knowledge and Ability to gather and create safe drinking water.

Documents:

- Small Bible
- Small copy of Declaration of Independence and US Constitution with Bill of Rights
- Small survival field book
- And of course maps of locations you will be traveling in.

Chapter 15: Conclusion

This book may actually be the beginning of your Bug Out journey depending on how much you already know about prepping and survival. Now is the time to take massive action and get things done in advance. Not out of the spirit of fear, but out of the spirit of love using your sound mind that God has given you with logic and reason in as your guide.

We have covered a lot of subjects throughout this book yet to be quite honest we've only scratched the surface. I hope that you use this book as it's intended, to get you and your family as prepared as possible in the shortest amount of time.

Remember: Proper Planning Prevents Problems.

Special Gift

God has a Gift for You!   The Plan of Salvation:

There is no formal prayer of salvation as many churches would have you believe, God's Word is very clear - there is only one way to get to the Father in heaven and that is through Jesus Christ (John 14:6). Jesus says that you must be born again to enter into heaven (John 3:3-5).

Salvation is simply the first step in building an open and honest relationship with God. We all have sinned and fall short every day, but there is Hope in Jesus Christ - Just cry out to God in sincerity and honesty asking for forgiveness and for Him to Save you, Sanctify you, and fill you with His Holy Spirit - Ask for His will to be done in your life on earth as it is in Heaven and That's it, now just keep it real with God.

A Warning:

The Christian walk is not an easy life on the surface. The Word of God says that we will be hated in all the world for Christ namesake (Matt. 24:9). The Bible says that in the last days are enemy prevail against us physically until Christ returns to save us (Dan 7:21, 22). Furthermore, we must endure hardship as a good soldier of Jesus Christ (2 Tim 2:3) and yet we are never alone in this, God promises us that He will never leave us nor forsake us if we believe in him (Matt.28:20).

In everything we go through we have the peace and joy of God which surpasses all understanding (Philp. 4:6-8) The Bible declares, "For I consider the sufferings of this present time are not worthy to be compared with the glory which shall be revealed in us". (Rom 8:18). However, in all these things we are more than conquerors through Jesus Christ (Rom. 8:37)

Stay In Contact

Our Contact Information

Stay in Contact with the American Christian Defense Alliance, Inc. Contactus@acdainc.org Or Email Us Though Our Website At: www.ACDAInc.Org

Join Our Mailing List

We also Greatly Appreciate You Signing Up For Our Mailing List and Providing a Good Rating and review for this Book. Your reviews help other people like yourself find this book on Amazon and benefit from its contents.

If You or Your Family have been Blessed by this book please let us know by dropping us a line through our website at http://acdainc.org

Thanks Again for Reading

God Bless!

Find All Our Books On Amazon

Our Books on Amazon:

Biblical Bug Out: Don't Bug In - Follow The Calling

Christian Prepping 101: How To Start Prepping

Prepping: A Christian Perspective

Prepping: Survival Basics

Real Men Don't Make Promises: Understanding Oaths, Pacts, Covenants & Promises From A Biblical Perspective

A Vague Notion: How To Overcome Limiting Beliefs of Fear and Anxiety Through the Word of God

Dirt on Your Tabies: 7 Short Stories of Seisho Ryu Ninjutsu

Salvation for Your Unsaved Mom: 10 Things to Tell Your Mom Before She Dies